LITERATURE CIRCLES

Using Student Interaction to Improve Reading Comprehension

Written by
Marcia C. Huber

Editor: Sheri Samoiloff
Illustrator: Jane Yamada
Cover Photographer: Michael Jarrett
Designers: Moonhee Pak and Terri Lamadrid
Cover Designer: Barbara Peterson
Art Director: Tom Cochrane
Project Director: Carolea Williams

Special thanks to my husband and children for having the patience to give me time to write.

Table of Contents

# Introduction

Literature circles are small groups of three to six students who meet together daily to read and discuss a piece of literature. The groups read novels that they choose from a variety of titles. Students also complete a variety of activities and projects related to their reading. Literature circles also work well with poems, short stories, and a single title chosen for the entire class. This book provides a proven, structured approach for conducting literature circles with all ages. Feel free to supplement your own literature ideas with the ideas suggested in this book.

Using literature circles in your classroom will benefit both you and your students in a variety of ways. The open-ended assignments in a literature circle unit allow you to meet the needs of students at all reading levels. This approach also provides numerous opportunities to assess each student's reading and writing skills. Literature circles challenge students to make choices about the literature they read. They learn to be responsible and accountable for these choices. The literature circle approach gives every student in your class a chance to read aloud daily, which improves reading skills such as decoding and the use of context clues to comprehend text. Students have the opportunity to form their own conclusions to questions. They feel successful and their self-esteem improves because they learn from listening to each other.

Literature Circles is an easy-to-use resource book that features
- step-by-step directions for teacher preparation
- tips for implementing literature circles
- a sample daily schedule—that can be adapted for use with any book—for the first time you conduct a literature circle unit
- a sample daily schedule for a literature circle unit on *Sarah, Plain, and Tall* to follow or use as a model to create your own unit schedule
- daily task questions and lesson ideas with coordinating reproducibles
- teacher and student assessment ideas with reproducible evaluation forms
- synopses of recommended books for grades 3–6 that also indicate the level of reading difficulty

Getting Started

U se the first four to six weeks of the school year to establish routines and get to know the skills and learning styles of your students. Use this time to conduct whole-class lessons that allow students to respond to and discuss a single piece of literature. Choose several activities for students to complete and discuss together. This will prepare them to work independently in literature circles. You will also want to explain the elements of a story such as characterization, setting, conflict, plot, climax, and solution. Discuss the theme of a story, and have students create a story map (see page 44) to practice identifying key elements of a story, retelling, and sequencing.

Choosing Books

When your students are ready for their first literature circle group, decide the number of students to have in each group and which books they will read. Groups of four to six students each work best. Choose books based on a theme you are teaching in your content areas. For example, themes may include ecology, nature, oceanography, courage, race relations, friendship, slavery, and periods of history such as the Civil War or the Colonial Period. When making your selections, try to find books of similar lengths. This way students will finish reading their novels close to the same time, making management easier. The Literature Selections section (pages 65–80) is an excellent resource to help you find appropriate books for your class. Collect four to six copies each of five or six titles that relate to your chosen theme.

To increase your literature circle book collection,
- use bonus points from book orders
- pair up with other teachers and share sets of books
- ask your school PTA or PTO group to help purchase books
- organize fund-raisers to earn money to purchase books
- ask parents to donate books

Because one class may be reading five or six different books at one time, many teachers are concerned that they may not be able to read all the books they offer students. Listed below are some reasons for reading books and alternatives if you can't read a book.

Reasons to read the books

1. You will be aware of problematic vocabulary.
2. You will be able to ask specific questions pertaining to a given section of that particular book.
3. You will be aware of any controversial material in the book.
4. You will be able to answer questions or help solve problems that may arise within the group because you will know the answers.

Alternatives if you can't read a book ahead of time

1. Choose books from the Literature Selections section or from a list of titles recommended by the local librarian, or use the Internet to search for Web sites that recommend children's books and provide brief synopses.
2. Listen to students read and discuss their books each day. You will soon know everything you need to about the books and more!
3. Be honest and tell students that you have not had a chance to read the books. Ask them to critique their books.
4. Ask students to summarize the content of various chapters and reflect often so you can gain additional knowledge about the books.

The purpose of literature circles is to have students discover answers for themselves with a little help from their peers. When students have a question, challenge them to find the answer by discussing their question with other group members or by looking back in the book.

Organizing Supplies

Several literature circle groups work simultaneously, each reading different novels and performing different tasks. Prepare students to be independent workers and organize student materials for independent access so that literature circles run smoothly. The key to creating successful literature circles (while maintaining your sanity) is organization. This section outlines a simple organizational system.

First, decide where you want your literature circle groups to meet. Arrange the classroom to suit your needs. Have students sit in clustered desks in the classroom or sit in clustered circles on the floor. If your school has an environment that allows students to work in the hall, invite one literature circle group to work there each day.

Next, create a folder for each student. Use file folders or fold construction paper in half and staple writing paper inside. Spiral notebooks or writing journals also work well.

Then, gather a plastic crate or cardboard file box for each group to store their work in. Include student folders, a group folder (file folder), and individual copies of the reading book in each crate or box. Assign each group a number, and label the crates or boxes and group folders accordingly.

Finally, create a supply center. A supply center is a small bookcase or table that contains the group crate or box and everything your students will need as they work on related activities and projects. Supplies may include

- construction paper
- tagboard
- sentence strips
- project ideas
- crayons or markers
- index cards
- glue
- rulers
- scissors
- paper scraps
- old magazines

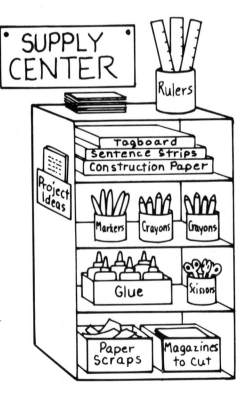

When students begin working on projects, add any materials they will need to the supply center. Model the proper procedure for handling materials and replacing them in the correct containers. Encourage students to get their own supplies so you may work uninterrupted with other groups.

Creating Schedules

Now that you have set up folders, chosen books, and organized groups, you are ready to plan your literature circle day. Each day may be slightly different. The literature circle concept allows flexibility with time and assignments. Choose assignments that best fit the needs of your students.

Decide how long and how often you want groups to meet. Literature circles can be conducted successfully in 40 minutes to an hour, three to five days a week. Each day, have students meet in their assigned groups and read seven to ten pages of their book, depending on the level of the book assigned and your students' reading ability. Have students complete a Question of the Day, a Skill of the Day assignment, and any evaluation forms you select. Choose any additional assignments you want students to focus on or conclude literature circles after students complete the Skill of the Day assignment. Have students complete the activities that best fit the time allotment you choose.

If a group does not complete an assignment in the time allotted, have the group members complete it at a later time during the day or take the novel home and complete the assignment at home. Try to keep students working at the same pace so each group will finish the unit at about the same time.

Introducing Literature Circles

After you select the five or six books to use, introduce the group roles, spend time modeling the roles, and then have students role-play them. Explain to the class that they will be starting a literature circle unit. Tell them that for the next three to six weeks they will work in groups to read one book they choose from your selection of books, discuss answers to questions about their book, complete assignments, and choose a culminating project to complete and share with classmates. Explain that students will take turns serving different roles each day. Also, discuss the importance of cooperative group work.

Explaining Roles

There are two required roles and four optional roles in a literature circle group. Decide whether or not to assign students the optional roles depending on your classroom dynamics and the maturity level of your students.

Required Roles

Leader The leader is in charge of the group. Students take turns being leader for the day in the order their name is listed on the group index card (see page 10). The leader decides the reading approach for the day. For example, students could read with a partner or take turns reading together, round-robin style. Always have students read orally, which allows group members to help each other decode difficult words. As one student reads aloud, the other group members read the words silently. After the groups read the assigned number of pages, the leader begins a discussion based on the Question of the Day (see pages 24–25) and helps everyone stay on task.

Listener Students listen to the directions the leader provides and to the other group members as they discuss the book and answer questions. All students other than the leader for the day are listeners even if you choose to assign students optional roles.

Generate with the class a list of "good leader" and "good listener" characteristics. Write their responses on chart paper. Display the charts at the front of the classroom. Invite students to role-play effective leaders and listeners.

☆ A Good Leader ☆
· is not bossy
· makes sure everyone par[...]
· leads the discussion
· calls on one person at [...]
· promotes cooperative[...]

☆ A Good Listener ☆
· looks at the person who is talking
· does not laugh or make fun of the person who is talking
· waits to be called upon before speaking
· participates
· uses good manners

Optional Roles

Manager   Person responsible for gathering the group crate or box and other necessary materials for the day from the supply center and returning them when the literature circle group completes its work each day.

Timer   Person responsible for keeping the group on task so work will be completed in the allotted time frame. Uses classroom clock to keep track of time.

Encourager   Person responsible for offering supportive comments that make group members feel comfortable as they share. For example, this person might say *I really enjoyed hearing your description of the main character* or *I really appreciate that you read with such expression.*

Summarizer   Person responsible for writing a summary about the pages read during that day's group meeting. Have the summarizer read the summary to the group at the beginning of the meeting the following day.

If you decide to assign students the optional roles, discuss the duties of these roles, and invite students to role-play them in front of the class.

Introducing Books and Setting Up Groups

Use the following steps to introduce novels to students:

- Discuss the theme you have chosen.
- Display a thematic poster or banner in your classroom.

- Hold books up one at a time, and read the title and author.
- Give a synopsis of each book, or read the summary from the back cover.
- Highlight intriguing features of each book to generate student interest.
- Ask each student to list on a piece of paper his or her top three book choices. Encourage students to choose wisely and not let classmates influence their decisions.
- Collect the papers, and use the lists to create five to six groups with four to six students in each group.

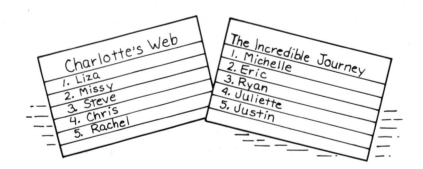

- Write the name of each book on the top of a separate index card. Number each card to show the number of students for that group. Try to place the same number of students in each group.
- Write students' names on the appropriate cards, giving as many first choices as possible. Check that students in each group will work well together.
- Announce each student's name and the book he or she will be reading.
- Explain that each student will create a literature circle folder before meeting in the group.

Creating Student Folders

Have students use one folder for all their literature circle units, or have them create a new folder before the start of each unit. Explain that they will record in their individual folder new characters, challenging vocabulary, and responses to the group discussion of each day's reading. Point out that this folder will also help you assess their understanding of the different story elements of their book and that you will randomly check the folders during the unit. Give each student a folder (see page 6), and have students follow these steps to customize their folder:

1. Give each student a copy of the selected book.
2. Have students write a title (e.g., *Literature Circles*) and their name on the front cover and number their pages.
3. Ask them to label the top of the first page *Title Page* and then write the title and the author of the book. Have them allow room at the bottom of the paper to write a prediction.
4. Have students label the top of pages two and three *Vocabulary Words*. Tell them they will record on these pages difficult or interesting words they find while reading.
5. Ask students to label the top of page four *Characters*. Tell them they will record on this page the names of the characters in the story and words or phrases the author uses to describe the characters.
6. Use the guidelines below to teach a lesson on how to write a prediction.

Tell students that a prediction involves thinking about what is known in the text and anticipating what will happen next. Point out that there are no wrong answers in predicting and having a prediction before reading is important because it helps extend your imagination. The more experiences students have with making predictions, the more they will think creatively of the possibilities that could exist given a set of circumstances. Have students choose one of the following ways to write a prediction about their story on page one of their folder:

- Look at the illustrations on the book cover and inside pages. Write a paragraph explaining what you think this book will be about (e.g., *I think this book will be about a puppy that gets lost.*).
- Write two or more questions that you would like to be able to answer as you read this book (e.g., *Will the puppy find its owner?*).

- Silently read the first page and answer each of the following questions:
  - Who is the book about?
  - What seems to be the problem in the story?
  - When does the story take place (past, present, future)?
  - Where does the story take place?

Participating in the First Meeting

Invite students to meet in their assigned groups. Explain and model proper use of the supply center, and invite students to role-play appropriate ways to retrieve and return materials.

Introduce the group crate or box, and explain its contents. Tell students it will be stored in the supply center and each manager or group leader (if optional roles are not used) is responsible for getting and returning the crate or box each day. Explain to students that they will find in their group folder any assignments the group is required to complete together and all the reproducibles they need. Invite group members to write their names on the front of the group folder.

Explain to students that all completed assignments are to be placed back in the group folder at the end of the literature circle meeting each day. Tell them that the group folder, student folders, and copies of the novel are to be placed back in the group crate or box each day.

Brainstorm with the class appropriate behavior and fair consequences for negative behavior during literature circles. List student responses on chart paper. If a member of the group is being disruptive, encourage the group leader to warn the student that he or she will be removed from the group if the negative behavior continues.

If a student continues to behave inappropriately after a warning is given, ask the leader to immediately remove the disruptive student from the group. Have the student go to a designated location in the classroom, preferably an isolated area. Have the student complete the assignment for the day without help from other group members.

Have students discuss with group members appropriate group behavior and brainstorm three rules they think are especially important. Have students write these rules on the Group Contract (page 13) and place the completed form inside the group folder. Students are now ready to begin reading and discussing their books in literature circle groups.

Group Contract

Brainstorm three rules you think are especially important for your literature circle group to run smoothly.

We, members of the _____ group, agree to do the following

(book title)

to make our group work:

1. _____

2. _____

3. _____

Signatures

1. _____   4. _____

2. _____   5. _____

3. _____   6. _____

Building and Implementing Literature Circles

Because literature circles make students responsible for running their groups, you will be free to rotate among the groups to assess progress and provide assistance as needed. Once students are familiar with the procedures of literature circles, you will spend less time explaining concepts because students will use the skills and knowledge they gained from previous literature circle units.

This section and the Assessment section (pages 41–64) provide a variety of resources to help you plan and successfully implement your literature circle units. Use the first sample schedule as a guide to help you set up any unit. The second sample schedule is for a unit on Patricia MacLachlan's *Sarah, Plain and Tall*. Use this unit with students who have completed at least one literature circle unit. Remember that the activities in the sample units are very flexible. Choose the activities that coordinate with your instructional goals, and present them in the order that best meets the needs of your students. The sample schedules reference the three main components of literature circles:

Students discuss and answer the **Question of the Day** (pages 24–25) to help them focus on the story elements of their book. Each day, choose from the list a question that is appropriate for the material students will read that day or create your own question, and write it on the chalkboard. Have each literature circle group discuss the question, and ask each group member to write the question and an answer in his or her student folder. As students become more experienced, have them answer more than one question each day.

Students focus on comprehension, vocabulary, and grammar skills in the **Skill of the Day** assignments (pages 26–40). Introduce a skill for the day, and invite students to complete the corresponding reproducible in their groups. Students of all reading levels can use the reproducibles with any book selection.

Students use a variety of **evaluation forms** to assess both individual progress and group work. These forms and a variety of informal and formal assessment ideas (e.g., book chats, individual projects) are discussed in greater detail in the Assessment section.

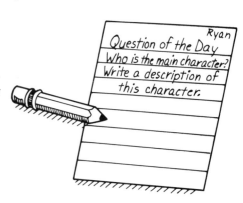

Sample Schedule

	Day 1	Day 2	Day 3
Preparation	• Decide on the theme of study. • Select five or six books that fit the theme and provide an appropriate range of difficulty.	• Select the number of books needed.	• Establish groups based on students' choices. • Prepare literature circle folders. • Prepare group crates or boxes and the supply center.
In the Lesson	• Explain the literature circle concept to the class. • Explain the roles assigned to students. • Discuss the roles of leader and listener. Discuss optional roles if you assign them to students. Brainstorm good leader and listener traits with the class on chart paper. • Model for the class or invite students to role-play the qualities of good leaders and listeners and responsibilities of students in optional roles.	• Introduce the books to the class. • Give students a brief, enthusiastic, descriptive synopsis of each book, or read aloud the summary from the back cover. • Have students write on a piece of paper three book titles they want to read. Stress the importance of choosing books that truly interest them. • Collect all the papers.	• Announce the members of each literature circle group, and distribute the books. • Have students set up their student folder. • Have students look at the cover of their book, read the first page, and look at any pictures. • Explain the literature circle management system. Tell students that each group will have a crate or box in which to keep materials such as folders and books. • Have groups complete a Group Contract (page 13).

	Day 4	Day 5	Day 6
Preparation	• Decide the number of pages you want students to read. Assign all groups the same number of pages. • Write on the board the following Question of the Day: *How does the book begin?* • Choose a Skill of the Day assignment, and copy a class set of the coordinating reproducible. Place a set of reproducibles in each group folder. • Copy a class set of the Leader Evaluation and Teamwork Evaluation forms (page 47), and place a set of reproducibles in each group folder.	• Decide the number of pages you want students to read. Assign all groups the same number of pages. • Write on the board *Why do you think the author chose to begin the story this way?* • Choose a Skill of the Day assignment, and copy a class set of the coordinating reproducible. Place a set of reproducibles in each group folder.	• Decide the number of pages you want students to read. Assign all groups the same number of pages. • Write on the board *Who is the main character(s) in your book?* • Choose a Skill of the Day assignment, and copy a class set of the coordinating reproducible. Place a class set of reproducibles in each group folder. • Copy a class set of the Self-Evaluation form (page 48), and place a set of reproducibles in each group folder.
In the Lesson	• Invite the manager or leader (if you do not use optional roles) to get the group crate or box. • Ask the leader to choose the reading style for the day. • Have students read the assigned number of pages and list any new characters or challenging vocabulary in their student folder. • Invite them to discuss how the book begins. • After students listen to group members share answers, have them write their answer in their student folder. • Have students complete the Skill of the Day assignment. • Ask the groups to fill out the Leader Evaluation and Teamwork Evaluation forms. • Have students place all completed work in their group folder, place all books and folders in the group crate or box, and place the crate or box in the supply center.	• Invite the manager to get the group crate or box. • Ask the leader to choose the reading style for the day. • Have students add to their character and vocabulary pages as they read. • Have them discuss why they feel the author chose to begin the book the way he or she did. • After students listen to group members share answers, have them write their answer in their student folder. • Have them complete the Skill of the Day assignment. • Have groups place all completed work, folders, and books in their group crate or box, and place the crate or box in the supply center.	• Invite the manager to get the group crate or box. • Ask the leader to choose the reading style for the day. • Have students add to their character and vocabulary pages as they read. • Have them discuss the main character(s) in the story. • Invite group members to answer the discussion question in their student folder. • Have students complete the Skill of the Day assignment. • Invite them to complete the Self-Evaluation form. • Have groups place all completed work, folders, and books in their group crate or box, and place the crate or box in the supply center.

16

Building and Implementing Literature Circles

	Day 7	Day 8	Day 9
Preparation	• Decide the number of pages you want students to read. Assign all groups the same number of pages. • Write on the board *Where is the setting of your story?* • Find several examples of well-written story settings. • Choose a Skill of the Day assignment, and copy a class set of the coordinating reproducible. Place a set of reproducibles in each group folder.	• Decide the number of pages you want students to read. Assign all groups the same number of pages. • Write on the board *What is the conflict or problem in your book?* • Choose a Skill of the Day assignment, and copy a class set of the coordinating reproducible. Place a set of reproducibles in each group folder. • Copy a class set of the Leader Evaluation form (page 47), and place a set of reproducibles in each group folder.	• Decide the number of pages you want students to read. Assign all groups the same number of pages. • Write on the board *What is the theme of the story or the author's message?* • Choose a Skill of the Day assignment, and copy a class set of the coordinating reproducible. Place a set of reproducibles in each group folder. • Copy a class set of the Self-Evaluation form (page 48), and place a set of reproducibles in each group folder.
In the Lesson	• Have students add to their character and vocabulary pages as they read. • Have them discuss the importance of using descriptive words (adjectives) to describe the setting. Tell students that the reader needs to be able to form a mental picture of the setting. • Read aloud several examples of well-written story settings. • Have students describe their own story's setting in their student folder. • Discuss the importance of avoiding "overused words" (e.g., good, nice, beautiful). Explain that using descriptive words helps form mental pictures in the reader's mind. • Have each group make a list of descriptive words used by the author to describe the story's setting. • Invite students to complete the Skill of the Day assignment. • Have groups place all completed work, folders, and books in their group crate or box, and place the crate or box in the supply center.	• Have students add to their character and vocabulary pages as they read. • Have them discuss the problem or conflict in the story and write their answer in their student folder. • Invite students to complete the Skill of the Day assignment. • Tell them to complete the Leader Evaluation form. • Have groups place all completed work, folders, and books in their group crate or box, and place the crate or box in the supply center.	• Have students add to their character and vocabulary pages as they read. • Have them discuss the theme of the story or what the author's message is and write their answer in their student folder. • Invite them to complete the Skill of the Day assignment. • Tell students to complete the Self-Evaluation form. • Have groups place all completed work, folders, and books in their group crate or box, and place the crate or box in the supply center.

Building and Implementing Literature Circles

	Day 10	Day 11	Day 12
Preparation	• Decide the number of pages you want students to read. Assign all groups the same number of pages. • Write on the board *Would you like to be a character in this book? Explain why and give many details.* • Choose a Skill of the Day assignment, and copy a class set of the coordinating reproducible. Place a set of reproducibles in each group folder.	• Decide the number of pages you want students to read. Assign all groups the same number of pages. • Write on the board *Tell about the conflict or the basic struggle in this story. Is the conflict between two characters, one character versus him/herself, a character and society, or a character and nature?* • Choose a Skill of the Day assignment, and copy a class set of the coordinating reproducible. Place a set of reproducibles in each group folder. • Copy a class set of the Self-Evaluation form (page 48), and place a set of reproducibles in each group folder.	• Decide the number of pages you want students to read. Assign all groups the same number of pages. • Write on the board *If you were the main character of the story, would you make similar decisions to the ones he or she made? Explain your answer.* • Choose a Skill of the Day assignment, and copy a class set of the coordinating reproducible. Place a set of reproducibles in each group folder. • Copy a class set of the Leader Evaluation form (page 47), and place a set of reproducibles in each group folder.
In the Lesson	• Have students add to their character and vocabulary pages as they read. • Have them discuss if they would like to be a character in their book. Have them explain why and give many details and then write their answer in their student folder. • Invite students to complete the Skill of the Day assignment. • Have groups place all completed work, folders, and books in their group crate or box, and place the crate or box in the supply center.	• Have students add to their character and vocabulary pages as they read. • Have them discuss the conflict or the basic struggle in their story and then write their answer in their student folder. • Invite students to complete the Skill of the Day assignment. • Tell them to complete the Self-Evaluation form. • Have groups place all completed work, folders, and books in their group crate or box, and place the crate or box in the supply center.	• Have students add to their character and vocabulary pages as they read. • Have them discuss the main character of the story and evaluate the decisions he or she made. • Have students write their answer in their student folder. • Invite them to complete the Skill of the Day assignment. • Tell students to complete the Leader Evaluation form. • Have groups place all completed work, folders, and books in their group crate or box, and place the crate or box in the supply center.

Building and Implementing Literature Circles

	Day 13	Day 14	Day 15
Preparation	• Gather various story summaries. • Decide the number of pages you want students to read. Assign all groups the same number of pages. • Write on the board **What is the climax** *(the most exciting part) of the story?*	• Decide the number of pages you want students to read. Assign all groups the same number of pages. • Write on the board **What does this story mean to you?** • Choose several activities and project ideas from Quick and Easy Activities (page 44), Responding through Writing (page 45), and Project Idea Cards (page 45). • Choose a Skill of the Day assignment, and copy a class set of the coordinating reproducible. Place a set of reproducibles in each group folder.	• Add any necessary materials to the supply center.
In the Lesson	• Have students add to their character and vocabulary pages as they read. • Have students discuss the climax of the story. • Have students write their answer in their student folder. • Discuss how to write a summary. Explain that a summary is brief and to the point. Read some summaries to the class. Tell students to include only the significant facts in a summary. • Have students write in paragraph form a summary that includes five meaningful events that have happened in the story so far. Have them write the events in the order in which they occurred in the story. • Have groups place all completed work, folders, and books in their group crate or box, and place the crate or box in the supply center.	• Invite groups who have finished their book to read their prediction from page one of their student folder and discuss how accurate it was. • Have the remaining groups read the assigned number of pages and discuss what the story means to them. • Invite students to write their answer in their student folder. • Have students complete the Skill of the Day assignment. • Introduce the activity and project ideas you selected. Explain to students they will complete activities and projects to share with the class. • Have students choose a project to complete from the Project Idea Cards.	• Have students work on activity and project assignments for the following few weeks.

Sample Schedule for *Sarah, Plain and Tall* by Patricia MacLachlan

In the following sample unit, the *Teacher* section outlines teacher preparation for each day and the *Students* section lists actions the students complete. Copy a class set of coordinating reproducibles and evaluation forms each day, and place them in each group folder.

	Day 1	Day 2	Day 3
Teacher	• Introduce *Sarah, Plain and Tall* and other book choices. • Create individual student and group folders.	• Write on the board the following Question of the Day: *Does the main character seem to be a real person? Tell why or why not.* • Skill of the Day—Introduce the Vocabulary Matrix reproducible (page 35).	• Write on the board the following Question of the Day: *Is the setting important to the story, or could this story take place anywhere?* • Skill of the Day—Introduce the Vocabulary Share reproducible (page 36).
Students	• Write names on the group folder. • Create a title page and character page. • Label pages to record vocabulary words and character notes. • Read seven pages in their group.	• Read seven pages as a group. • Leader leads discussion, focusing on the Question of the Day. • Write the answer to the Question of the Day in their student folder. • Add any new words to their vocabulary and character pages. • Complete the Skill of the Day assignment. • Complete the Leader Evaluation and Teamwork Evaluation forms (page 47).	• Read seven pages as a group. • Leader leads discussion, focusing on the Question of the Day. • Write the answer to the Question of the Day in their student folder. • Add any new words to their vocabulary and character pages. • Play a game of Concentration with the Vocabulary Share boxes cut apart. • Complete the Group Evaluation and Self-Evaluation forms (page 48).

	Day 4	**Day 5**	**Day 6**
Teacher	• Write on the board the following Question of the Day: *What problem does the main character face?* • Read with groups or struggling readers. • Skill of the Day—Introduce the Noun Review reproducible (page 37). • Collect work from group and student folders to check and write comments.	• Write on the board the following Question of the Day: *Does the setting influence the mood the author is trying to create?* • Skill of the Day—Introduce the Verb Review reproducible (page 38). • Hold book chats with two to three groups. • Complete the Teacher's Checklist for Group Evaluation form (page 46).	• Write on the board the following Question of the Day: *What is the most important idea, message, or lesson the author is trying to get across in the story?* • Skill of the Day—Introduce the Adjective Review reproducible (page 39). • Read with two to three groups of students.
Students	• Read seven pages as a group. • Leader leads discussion, focusing on the Question of the Day. • Write the answer to the Question of the Day in their student folder. • Add any new words to their vocabulary and character pages. • Complete the Skill of the Day assignment.	• Read seven pages as a group. • Leader leads discussion, focusing on the Question of the Day. • Write the answer to the Question of the Day in their student folder. • Add any new words to their vocabulary and character pages. • Complete the Skill of the Day assignment. • Complete the Leader Evaluation and Teamwork Evaluation forms (page 47).	• Read seven pages as a group. • Leader leads discussion, focusing on the Question of the Day. • Write the answer to the Question of the Day in their student folder. • Add any new words to their vocabulary and character pages. • Complete the Skill of the Day assignment.

	Day 7	Day 8	Day 9
Teacher	• Write on the board the following Question of the Day: *Compare the setting of the story to where you live. Which setting do you prefer, the story setting or your real-life setting? Why?* • Skill of the Day—Introduce the Adverb Review reproducible (page 40). • Hold book chats with two to three groups.	• Write on the board the following Question of the Day: *What is the climax (the most exciting part) of the story?* • Skill of the Day—Introduce the Story Clues reproducible (page 29).	• Skill of the Day—Introduce the Story Wheel reproducible (page 34). • Conduct a book chat with two to three groups. • Collect work from group and student folders to check and write comments.
Students	• Read seven pages as a group. • Leader leads discussion, focusing on the Question of the Day. • Write the answer to the Question of the Day in their student folder. • Add any new words to their vocabulary and character pages. • Complete the Skill of the Day assignment. • Complete the Group Evaluation and Self-Evaluation forms (page 48).	• Finish reading *Sarah, Plain and Tall.* • Leader leads discussion, focusing on the Question of the Day. • Write the answer to the Question of the Day in their student folder. • Add any new words to their vocabulary and character pages. • Complete the Skill of the Day assignment.	• Leader leads discussion, summarizing the story. • Write a summary in their student folder. • Complete the Skill of the Day assignment. • Complete the Leader Evaluation and Teamwork Evaluation forms (page 47).

	Day 10	Day 11	Day 12	Day 13	Day 14	Day 15
Teacher	• Skill of the Day—Introduce the Story Map reproducible (page 49).	• Gather drawing paper for Flip Books (see page 44). • Skill of the Day—Introduce the Flip Book reproducible (page 50).	• Skill of the Day—Introduce the Dynamic Book Report reproducible (page 52).	• Skill of the Day—Introduce the Responding through Writing reproducible (page 55).	• Decide amount of time allotted for students to complete projects. • Gather any needed supplies. • Skill of the Day—Introduce the Project Idea Cards (pages 56–64).	• Assess completed assignments and work in student folders.
Students	• Work in groups to complete a story map. • Share completed story map with the class.	• Make a flip book that shows the sequence of the major events in *Sarah, Plain and Tall.*	• Write a book report for *Sarah, Plain and Tall.*	• Complete an individual activity and share it with the class.	• Choose a project to complete. • Begin the project.	• Finish the project and share it with the class.

Question of the Day

Use the Question of the Day to have students focus on the elements of their story. Each day, choose a question from the list below or create one of your own, and write it on the chalkboard. Have each literature circle group discuss the question, and ask each group member to write an answer in his or her student folder.

Character Questions

1. Who is the main character? Write a description of this character.
2. Does the main character seem to be a real person? Tell why or why not.
3. How are you like or different from the main character in this story?
4. What problem does the main character face?
5. What is the main character's main goal?
6. How many supporting characters does the author include in the story? Which characters support (or oppose) the main character?
7. Does the main character change over the course of the story? How?
8. Would you like to be a character in this story? Which one? Why?
9. Describe the way of life of the main character. How does this character occupy his or her time each day? How does his or her way of life compare to yours?
10. If you were the main character of the story, would you make similar decisions to the ones he or she made? Explain your answer.

Setting Questions

1. Does the setting influence the mood the author is trying to create? Explain your answer.
2. Describe the setting in detail.
3. How is the setting necessary for plot development?
4. Does the author use many descriptive words to describe the setting? Name some of the words.
5. Does weather play an important role in the story? Explain your answer.
6. Is the setting important to the story, or could this story take place anywhere?
7. Compare the setting of the story to where you live. Which setting do you prefer, the story setting or your real-life setting? Why?
8. Does your story take place in a real location? Explain your answer.
9. When does the story take place? What year or period of history do you think the author is writing about? What clues are given in the story?
10. If you could change the setting of the story, where would you change it to? Why?

Theme Questions

1. What is the most important idea, message, or lesson the author is trying to get across in the story?
2. Is the theme clearly stated or is it implied? Give an example.
3. What does the story mean to you?
4. Does this story have one theme or several? What is the theme(s)?
5. Why do you think the author chose to tell this story? What is the most important idea we are supposed to remember?

Plot Questions

1. What is the climax (the most exciting part) of the story?
2. What is the conflict or problem to be solved?
3. How is the problem solved?
4. List several events that lead up to the climax.
5. Tell about the conflict or the basic struggle in this story. Is the conflict between two characters, one character versus him/herself, a character and society, or a character and nature?

Skill of the Day

Literature circles are especially tailored to strengthen reading comprehension skills. The Skill of the Day reproducibles (pages 28–40) allow you to target specific skills for students to practice. Copy a class set of the reproducible page you decide to use each day, and place a set in each group folder. Many of the reproducibles can be used again at different stages of a story. Have students complete the reproducibles independently. Read the following descriptions to decide which reproducibles meet the needs of your students.

Comprehension

Identifying the Main Idea—When the reader identifies the main idea, he or she determines the focus or theme of a story. The reader sees how the details of the story work together to support one idea. The Shed Some Light on These Story Facts reproducible (page 28) helps students to identify the main idea in the story.

Characterization—To comprehend the story, readers must understand the characters. Good readers recognize the traits of the characters, understand what they do and why, and identify their role in the overall meaning of the story. Characterization is a skill most useful in narrative text, but the same need for understanding is present when studying biographies or individuals in history. The Story Clues reproducible (page 29) encourages students to become detectives to learn more about a specific character in their story.

Sequencing—Sequencing is the ability to put objects, activities, and events in a logical order. Good readers see the big picture of the story instead of focusing on individual details. The Story Illustrations reproducible (page 30) challenges students to draw scenes from the story in the proper sequence.

Making Connections—A key element of reading comprehension is connecting what the reader knows to what he or she reads. Learning becomes real when the reader makes connections to his or her personal experiences. Good readers compare what they read to their own view of themselves, their perceptions of the world around them, and other prior knowledge. The Fly High with Books! reproducible (page 31) and the Bright Ideas reproducible (page 32) help students connect their story with events that happen in everyday life. Invite students to complete these reproducibles once they have finished their book.

Retelling—Retelling is the ability to summarize and organize the elements of a story. Good readers process the key points of the text and explain those points in their own words. Good listening skills are an important part of this strategy. The Story Steps reproducible (page 33) and Story Wheel reproducible (page 34) give students practice summarizing and organizing the elements of the story.

Vocabulary

Synonyms and Antonyms—Good writers use synonyms and antonyms when they want to vary their word choice and analyze the meaning of words. The Vocabulary Matrix reproducible (page 35) challenges students to analyze the meaning of selected words from their book.

Word Meaning—Good readers discover the hidden or special significance in a word. The Vocabulary Share reproducible (page 36) provides a unique way for students to play a role in discovering the meaning of a particularly important word from their story.

Grammar

Literature circles also provide opportunities for students to study syntax. Students become more proficient readers when they understand language rules. Use the following reproducibles to have students identify different parts of speech as they read.

Nouns—The Noun Review reproducible (page 37) asks students to identify and record different types of nouns in their story.

Verbs—The Verb Review reproducible (page 38) challenges students to find and list verbs in their book.

Adjectives—The Adjective Review reproducible (page 39) asks students to identify and record adjectives in their story.

Adverbs—The Adverb Review reproducible (page 40) challenges students to find and list adverbs in their story.

Name _____ Date _____

Shed Some Light on These Story Facts

Write a summary of the story facts for your book.

Title _____

Author _____

Characters

_____

_____

_____

_____

Setting

_____

_____

_____

_____

Main Idea of the Story

_____

_____

_____

_____

Name _____ Date _____

Story Clues

Be a reading detective. Answer each question about the book you are reading. Make sure to focus on the main events.

Title _____

Author _____

Who is the main character? _____

_____

What did the main character do? _____

_____

When was this done? _____

_____

Why did the main character do this? _____

_____

Where did the main character do it? _____

_____

How was it done? _____

_____

What was the main character's overall role in the story? _____

_____

Building and Implementing Literature Circles

Name _____ Date _____

Story Illustrations

Choose four important events that have occurred in your book so far. Illustrate each event in the proper sequence below. Write one complete sentence to describe each scene.

Title _____

Author _____

1.	2.

3.	4.

Name _____ Date _____

Fly High with Books!

Answer these questions about the book you read.

Title _____

Author _____

From whose point of view is the story told? Support your answer.

_____

_____

_____

Choose a new title for this story. Explain why you made this choice.

_____

_____

_____

Compare this book with others you have read on the same topic. How would you rate this book? Create a rating scale.

_____

_____

_____

Did you like the way the book ended? Tell why or why not. How would you have chosen to write the ending?

_____

_____

_____

Name _____ Date _____

Bright Ideas

Choose a bright idea to complete.

Title _____

Author _____

- Write a critique of the book. Would you recommend this book to a friend? Explain your answer with specific reasons.

- Do you think the main character makes wise decisions? Tell why or why not. Support your answer with information from the book.

- Should schools require students to read this book? Tell why or why not.

- Write a poem based on the characters and main events in this story.

- Write a newspaper article about an event that takes place in this story.

_____

_____

_____

_____

_____

_____

_____

_____

_____

_____

Name _____ Date _____

Story Steps

Use the scale shown at right to rate your book. Write the story elements in complete sentences.

Title _____

Author _____

Solution:

Event:

Event:

Event:

Problem:

Setting:

Characters:

Rating (circle one)
Reading this book is:

Easy   Just Right   Challenging

Name _____ Date _____

Story Wheel

Draw a picture or write a complete sentence to summarize each story element.

Title _____

Author _____

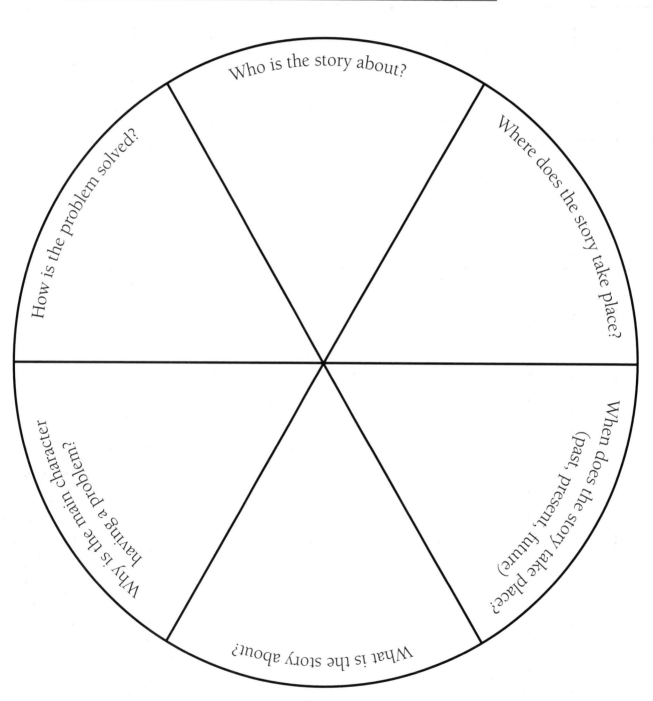

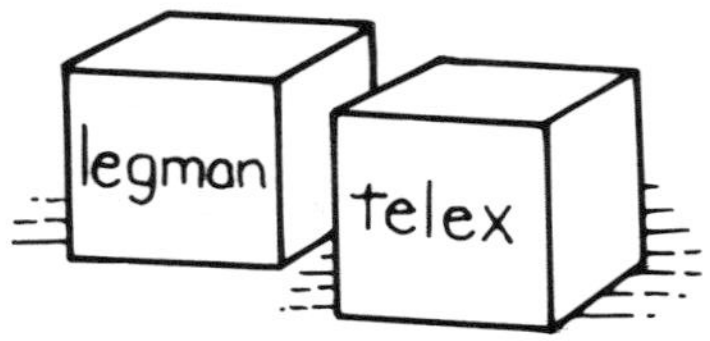

Vocabulary Matrix

A vocabulary matrix is another way to learn more about words in the story. In the first column, write eight words from the book you are reading that you do not already know and that are critical to understanding the story. In the next two columns, write a synonym and an antonym of each word, if possible. In the last column, write the definition of each vocabulary word as it relates to the story. Underline the key words in the definition.

Title _____

Author _____

Vocabulary Word	Synonym	Antonym	Definition

Building and Implementing Literature Circles

Name _____ Date _____

Vocabulary Share

Write a word that is important to the understanding of the story in the first box. Make sure all group members select a different word. Trade papers with group members. Have each person fill in one of the other sections by illustrating the word, writing the definition, or writing a sentence using the word. Collect your paper. Cut apart the boxes. Place all group members' pieces together and play a game of Concentration or Memory.

Title _____

Author _____

Example

Word orchard	Definition a planting (or grove) of fruit trees
Word in a Sentence We picked apples in the apple <u>orchard</u>.	Picture 

Word	Definition
Word in a Sentence	**Picture**

Name _____ Date _____

Noun Review

Nouns are words that name people, places, things, and ideas. Find a total of 15 nouns as you read your book today. Record each noun in the correct column below.

Title _____

Author _____

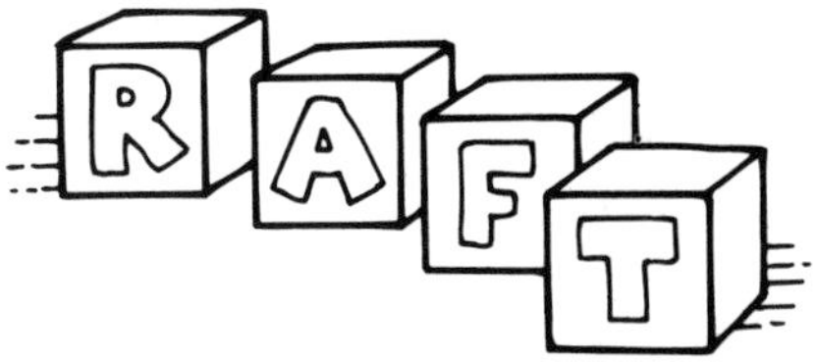

Person	Place	Thing	Idea
grandma	Tennessee	raft	freedom

Building and Implementing Literature Circles

Name _____ Date _____

Verb Review

Verbs are words that tell what action the noun is doing. Find 15 verbs as you read your book today. Record them below.

Title _____

Author _____

gathered	

Name _____ Date _____

Adjective Review

Adjectives are words that describe or modify nouns. Adjectives tell which one, how many, and what kind. Find 15 adjectives as you read your book today. Record each adjective in the first column and write the noun it describes in the second column.

Title _____

Author _____

Adjective	Noun Described
wooden	raft

Name _____ Date _____

Adverb Review

Adverbs are words that tell how, when, or where the action takes place. Many adverbs end with the letters *ly*. Find a total of 15 adverbs as you read your book today. Record each adverb in the correct column below.

Title _____

Author _____

How	When	Where
slowly	now	outside

Literature Circles © 2001 Creative Teaching Press

Assessment

L literature circles give students opportunities to respond to literature individually, in pairs, or in groups. Since all students do not learn at the same pace, literature circles are a great way for students to work in a non-threatening environment and help each other succeed. You have many choices for what areas of student learning you want to assess. Assess student progress throughout the literature unit and after a story is completed. This section features informal and formal assessment ideas to help you decide what and how much to grade.

Informal Assessment

As you rotate among the groups to listen to students read and discuss their books, conduct informal assessments. Note whether students are on task and working together to complete the day's activities. If a group is struggling with a Question of the Day or a Skill of the Day activity, provide help to get them back on track. If you notice that a group is reading more slowly than the rest, read a page to help them catch up. Use book chats to evaluate each group member's knowledge of a story and take active steps to help any students who are struggling with the book.

Book Chats

One way for you to assess student comprehension of the story being read is to visit each group as they complete their reading for the day or finish their book and conduct a book chat. A book chat will let you know immediately if students understand the story. Prepare for book chats by writing each of the following questions on a separate tongue depressor or craft stick:

- Is the book easy, just right, or challenging? Explain your answer.
- Name any other books you have read by this author.
- Tell about the main characters in your book.
- What part of the book do you like best? Why?
- Is the vocabulary the author is using easy to understand? Why or why not?
- How would you rate this book on a scale of 1 to 10? (1 = poor and 10 = great) Why?
- Would you recommend this book to a friend? Why or why not?
- If you could be one of the characters in your book, who would you be? Why?
- If you could change one event in the book, what event would you change? How would you make it different?
- Would you be interested in reading a different book by this author? Why or why not?

Keep the tongue depressors or craft sticks in a can, and take the can with you as you visit each group. Pass the can around the circle. Have each student remove a stick and read the question aloud to the group. Then, have the student answer it. Have students continue passing the can around the group until they have answered all of the questions.

Struggling Readers

Encourage a struggling reader to be a good listener and read when he or she feels comfortable. As the student begins to feel more confident, encourage him or her to read a sentence or a paragraph during his or her turn. If the group is partner reading, be the student's reading partner for the day. Help the student track words in the story and understand the key elements. Give positive reinforcement to build the student's self-confidence. Or, pair the student up with a competent reader, and have the struggling reader listen as his or her partner reads the story.

Teach a reading strategies mini-lesson to struggling readers. Present the following strategies:
- When you get stuck reading a word, skip the word and go on. Then go back to try again.
- When a word is unclear, backtrack and read it again.
- When you think a word does not make sense, read it again.
- When you see a new word, say the first sound, finish the sentence, and then say the word.

Formal Assessment

The following pages describe four different types of formal assessment both you and your students can use during and following literature circle units. Students try harder when they are aware that you are observing their behavior and participation. It is also important to teach students how to evaluate themselves and other group members. Have students complete activities and a culminating project as a means of demonstrating their knowledge of their book as well as giving an individual response to it.

Evaluation Forms

As you observe each group, use the Teacher's Checklist for Group Evaluation to keep a running record of student growth throughout the unit. Teach students how to complete the Leader Evaluation, Teamwork Evaluation, Group Evaluation, and Self-Evaluation forms. Have them practice completing these forms before they begin their first literature circle unit. Ask students to complete the forms on a daily or weekly basis. A good rule of thumb is to have students complete at least two forms each week. Feel free to create your own evaluation forms based on the class list of appropriate behavior and characteristics of good leaders and listeners or on student performance during optional roles. Listed below are short descriptions of each evaluation form.

Teacher Form
- The Teacher's Checklist for Group Evaluation (page 46) helps track students during group time.

Student Forms
- The Leader Evaluation (page 47) informs you how the leader did for the day.
- The Teamwork Evaluation (page 47) tracks each group's performance for the day.
- The Group Evaluation (page 48) helps students to assess their group's behavior.
- The Self-Evaluation (page 48) provides you with feedback on how each student feels he or she performed that day.

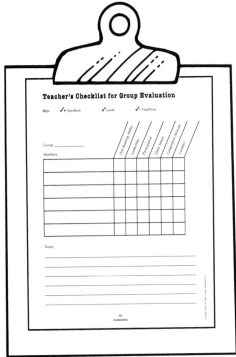

Quick and Easy Activities

As students finish reading their books, have individual students or groups complete one or several of the activities. Each activity idea comes with a corresponding reproducible. Invite groups to present their completed activity to the class one individual or group at a time.

Story Maps

Story maps help students break down the elements in any story. Give each group member a Story Map reproducible (page 49), or give each group a

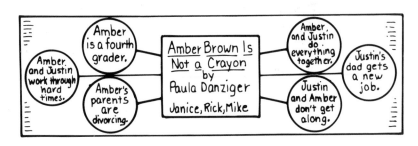

large piece of new or recycled (from your bulletin board) butcher paper. Have groups create a story map (graphic organizer) using the format from the reproducible to either write or draw the main events in their story.

Flip Books

Invite students to use the Flip Book reproducible (page 50) to retell the main events of their story.

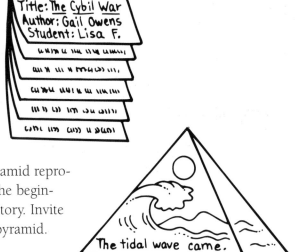

Story Pyramids

Have students use the Story Pyramid reproducible (page 51) to sequence the beginning, middle, and end of their story. Invite them to share their completed pyramid.

Dynamic Book Report

Ask students to follow the guidelines on the Dynamic Book Report reproducible (page 52) to write a three-paragraph report.

Student-Made Test

Give each student a Student-Made Test reproducible (pages 53–54). Challenge students to use the guidelines on the reproducible to create test questions. Have students also create an answer key. Use the test questions to assess the test creator's knowledge of the story. Use the answer keys to grade the tests. Use questions from the student-made tests to create a revised test for each group.

Responding through Writing

Have each student choose a writing activity from the Responding through Writing reproducible (page 55) when you have a limited amount of time but would like your students to combine higher-level thinking strategies and their creativity in their work.

Project Idea Cards

Copy and cut apart a set of Project Idea Cards (pages 56–64) for each student or pair of students. Have each student or pair choose one project to complete. Encourage students to share completed projects with the class. Collect the cards, and store each set in a separate resealable plastic bag for the next literature circle unit.

Teacher's Checklist for Group Evaluation

Key: ✔+ Excellent ✔ Good ✔- Fair/Poor

Group _____

Members

	Oral Reading Ability	Leadership	Participation	Quiet Voices	Cooperative Attitude	Conduct

Notes

_____

_____

_____

_____

_____

Literature Circles © 2001 Creative Teaching Press

Leader Evaluation

GOOD
SUPER

Name _____

Group _____

Date _____

1. Do you think the leader led the group well today? _____

2. What is one thing the leader did well today? _____

3. How can the leader improve? _____

4. How did the group listeners do today? _____

5. Did the group accomplish the work it was responsible for today? _____

_____

WONDERFUL • TERRIFIC

- -

Teamwork Evaluation

GREAT!

Name _____

Group _____

Date _____

Today we worked on _____ as a team.

One thing we did especially well was _____ .

One thing we need to work on is _____ .

We can accomplish this goal by _____ .

DYNAMITE

Group Evaluation

Name _____

Group _____

Date _____

Grade your group as a team. Use the grading scale below to evaluate your group's skills so far.

A = Excellent   B = Very Good   C = Average   D = Fair   F = Poor

Leadership Skills = _____

Listening Skills = _____

Participation = _____

Cooperation = _____

Conduct = _____

Quiet Voices = _____

- -

Self-Evaluation

Name _____

Date _____

Circle the best answer to describe your behavior in the group today.

Today I was the   leader   listener.

My conduct was   excellent   good   fair   poor.

My participation was   excellent   good   fair   poor.

My listening skills were   excellent   good   fair   poor.

My attitude was   excellent   good   fair   poor.

Story Map

Write or draw the main events in the story.

Title _____

Author _____

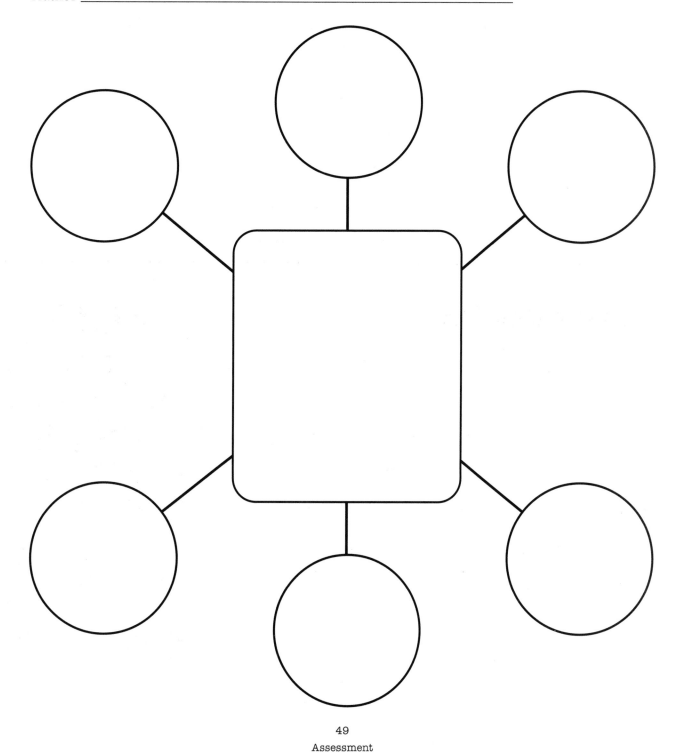

Flip Book

Materials

- 8" x 11" (21.5 cm x 28 cm) blank paper
- stapler
- crayons or markers

Directions

1. Place three sheets of paper on top of each other, and overlap as shown, leaving a 1" (2.5 cm) margin at the bottom of each page.

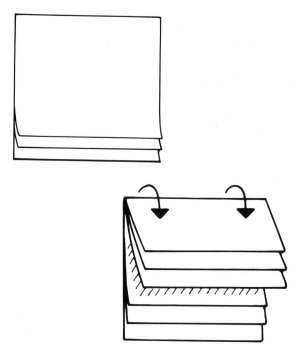

2. Hold the pages securely so they remain overlapped, and fold the top sheet so that its top edge folds to 1" above its bottom. The book now has six pages.

3. Staple through all layers at the fold. On the top page, write the title of the book, the author, and your name.

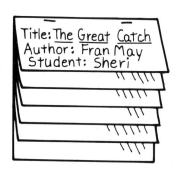

4. Illustrate and write about an important event from the story on each of the following five pages.

Literature Circles © 2001 Creative Teaching Press

Story Pyramid

Materials
- light-colored construction paper
- scissors
- crayons or markers
- glue

Directions

1. Cut a piece of light-colored construction paper into a 12" (30.5 cm) square.

2. Fold on the solid lines and cut on the dotted line. (see Diagram A)

3. Draw a picture in each of three sections to illustrate the beginning, middle, and end of the story. Label the beginning scene 1, the middle scene 2, and the last scene 3.

4. Write a caption at the bottom of each picture to tell the story. (see Diagram B)

5. Place glue on the blank section and stick it to the back of section 3 to form a pyramid shape. (see Diagram C)

6. Write the title and author of your book and your name on the inside of the pyramid.

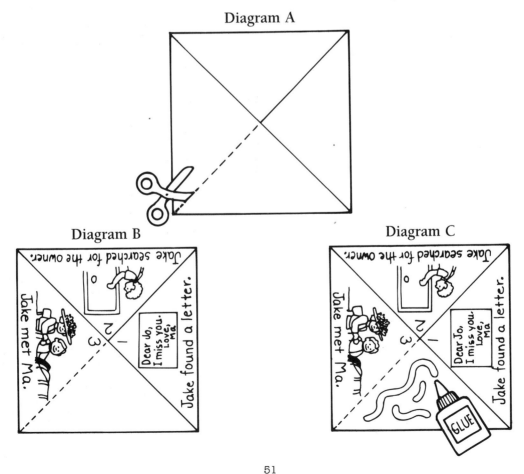

Diagram A

Diagram B

Diagram C

Literature Circles © 2001 Creative Teaching Press

Dynamic Book Report

A dynamic book report is composed of three paragraphs, knowledge of the story, and a little creativity. Follow the guidelines below to produce your masterpiece.

Top of the Page
Write the title and author of the book along with your name.

Paragraph One
Begin with a bang! The first sentence should grab the reader's attention. Describe each main character and the setting in the story. Write a minimum of five sentences in this paragraph.

Paragraph Two
Describe a significant event that takes place in your book. This may be your favorite event. Describe any conflicts in the story. Write a minimum of five sentences in this paragraph.

Paragraph Three
State your opinion of the book. Create a rating scale and use it to rate the book. Would you recommend this book for a particular audience? Tell why or why not. Write a minimum of five sentences in this paragraph.

Remember to include transition sentences to make your report flow smoothly.

Type or neatly write your book report.

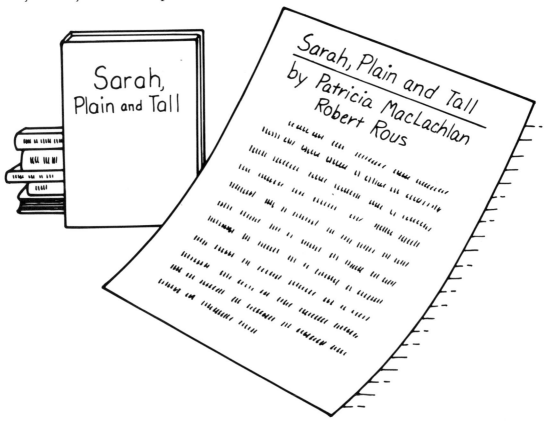

Literature Circles © 2001 Creative Teaching Press

Name _____ Date _____

Student-Made Test

Title _____

Author _____

Matching
List four important words from the story.

1. _____ 2. _____

3. _____ 4. _____

Write the definition of each important word listed above.

1. _____

_____

2. _____

_____

3. _____

_____

4. _____

_____

Fill in the Blank
Write four factual sentences about the story. Leave an important
word out of each sentence. Leave a blank space in place of the word.

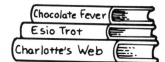

1. _____

2. _____

3. _____

4. _____

Student-Made Test

Multiple Choice
Write two multiple choice questions about the story. After each question, write one correct answer and two incorrect answers.

1. _____   2. _____

a. _____   a. _____

b. _____   b. _____

c. _____   c. _____

Essay Question
Write a question about the book you read that could be answered in one paragraph.

_____

_____

_____

_____

_____

Make an answer key for your test on another sheet of paper.

Literature Circles © 2001 Creative Teaching Press

Responding through Writing

Choose one of the following writing activities to complete. Share your completed activity with the class.

✓ Prepare a monologue from the story and perform it for the class.

✓ Give an oral description of an interesting character.

✓ Write a vivid description of an interesting character.

✓ Write at least three different endings for the story.

✓ Write about the saddest part of the story.

✓ Present a brief biography about the author.

✓ Give a synopsis of the story.

✓ Compare two books that you have read.

✓ Write new experiences, incidents, or adventures to add to the story.

✓ Give your personal reaction to one of the characters.

✓ Write a paragraph about the relationship between two characters.

✓ Choose a page and make a list of all the words that begin with a capital letter. Explain the capitalization rule for each word.

✓ Write a list of other titles for the story. Explain why you picked each title.

✓ After each chapter, write one or two sentences telling what happened in that chapter.

✓ Write three questions about the book and have a group member answer each question. Write down his or her answers.

✓ Make a chart of similarities between major and minor characters.

✓ Decide which character is your favorite and list reasons for your choice.

✓ Imagine that the main character can write a letter to another character. Write a letter from the main character (just after the first problem in the story) in which he or she explains the situation to another character.

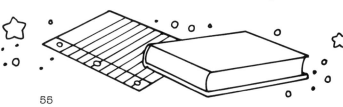

Project Idea Cards

Miniature Stage

Materials
- cardboard
- art supplies (e.g., tape or glue, scraps of paper and material)
- pipe cleaners or wire

Create a miniature "stage" from cardboard to show the setting of the story. Use art supplies and pipe cleaners to create the setting and main characters.

Book Jacket

Materials
- construction paper
- crayons, markers, or paint/paintbrushes

Use crayons, markers, or paint to design an original book jacket that shows your favorite part from the story. On the back of the jacket, write a summary of the book. Include your opinion of the book and whether or not you would recommend it.

New Endings

Materials
- writing paper
- props (optional)

Write three different endings to the story. Explain which ending you prefer and why. Act out one of the endings in front of the class.

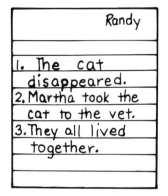

Musical Story

Materials
- musical instrument

Retell the story. Use an instrument to create sound effects.

Project Idea Cards

Dramatic Scene

Materials
- paper
- props (optional)

Write a script in which you change a scene from the story. Choose students to help you act out the new scene.

Fluffy:
Milo:
Tiger:
Fluffy:

Pantomime

Materials
- none

Act out a scene from the story using only body movements and facial expressions.

Word List

Materials
- drawing paper
- crayons or markers

Make a list of at least ten new, unusual, and interesting words from the story. After each word, write its definition and draw a picture to describe the word. Share the words, definitions, and pictures with the class. Then, use each word in a sentence.

rink
An enclosure for skating

Poster

Materials
- large paper or poster board
- paint/paintbrushes, crayons, chalk, or cut-out pictures
- glue (optional)

Choose your favorite scene from the story. Use paint/paintbrushes, crayons, chalk, or cut-out pictures to make a poster that describes the scene. Make the poster one-, two-, or three-dimensional. Include the book title on your poster.

The Velveteen Rabbit

Project Idea Cards

Letter Writing

Materials
- writing paper

Write a letter in which you recommend the book to a friend or librarian. Explain why you like or dislike the book.

Booklet

Materials
- construction paper
- crayons or markers

Make a booklet by folding a piece of construction paper into thirds. On the first section, write the book title, the author's name, and your name and draw a picture that describes the book. On the next section, write a summary about the book. On the third section, write an advertisement to sell the book to potential readers.

Flannel Board Story

Materials
- flannel pieces
- scissors
- flannel board

Use flannel pieces to make characters, scenery, and props in a scene from the story. Place the flannel board pieces on a flannel board as you retell the scene to the class.

Memory

Materials
- index cards

Write the name of each main character from the story on a separate index card. Write a description of each character on a separate card. Place all the cards together in a pile and shuffle them. Place the cards facedown in rows. Flip over two cards and see if the description card matches the character card. If they match, keep the cards in a pile. If they do not match, place the cards facedown where they were found. Continue trying to match cards until you have found all the matches.

Project Idea Cards

Diorama

Materials
- art supplies (e.g., shoe box, construction paper, colored pencils)
- index card
- glue (optional)

Turn a shoe box on its side. Use construction paper, colored pencils, crayons, or markers to make a scene from the story inside the shoe box. Describe the scene on an index card and attach the card to the back of the shoe box.

Model

Materials
- clay or plaster
- glue
- cardboard

Choose a scene from the book. Use clay or plaster to construct the scene. Glue the clay or plaster to a piece of cardboard. Share your completed model with the class.

Recipe

Materials
- writing paper

Write a recipe that reflects the tastes and personality of a character from the story. Include a list of ingredients and directions for making the recipe. Explain why this recipe reflects the taste of the character.

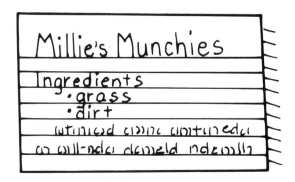

Painting

Materials
- paint/paintbrush
- white construction paper or canvas

Paint a picture of your favorite scene from the book on construction paper or canvas.

Project Idea Cards

Television

Materials
- medium-sized cardboard box
- scissors
- tape
- construction paper
- crayons or markers
- dowels

Cut out the front of a cardboard box. Cut large slits in both sides of the box. Tape pieces of construction paper together lengthwise. Draw four to six scenes from the book on the construction paper. Place the construction paper in the box and put each end through a slit on the side of the box. Tape each end of the paper to a dowel. Turn the dowels to change the scenes. Present the story in the form of a television program.

Dress Up

Materials
- clothing
- props

Dress as a character from the story and use props to act out a scene for the class.

Book Review Broadcast

Materials
- paper

Write a book review that includes a brief synopsis, a description of the main characters, your favorite part of the story, and why you liked or disliked the book. Broadcast the review to a "radio" audience.

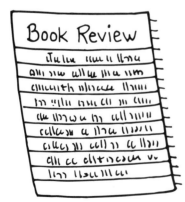

Puppet Show

Materials
- socks or craft sticks
- construction paper
- fabric scraps
- yarn
- markers
- glue

Use socks or craft sticks, construction paper, fabric scraps, yarn, and markers to make puppets that represent characters from the book. Present a puppet show to the class.

Literature Circles © 2001 Creative Teaching Press

Project Idea Cards

Time Line

Materials
- glue
- construction paper
- colored pencils, crayons, or markers

Glue sheets of construction paper together to make one long sheet. List the main events in the story in sequence to create a time line. Write positive events above the line and negative events below the line. Illustrate each event.

Comic Strip

Materials
- drawing paper
- pencil

Create a comic strip about the characters in the story. Use word bubbles when the characters are speaking.

Dolls

Materials
- dolls
- clothing
- index cards

Dress dolls as characters from the book. Write descriptions of who the dolls represent on index cards. Use the dolls and index cards to create a classroom display.

Photo Album

Materials
- drawing paper
- stapler
- crayons or markers

Fold a few pieces of paper in half. Staple through all pages on the fold. Make a photo album for one of the book's characters. Make a title for your album. Draw photos that would be found in the character's album. Write a description of each picture.

Project Idea Cards

Scrapbook

Materials
- construction paper
- stapler
- crayons or markers

Fold pieces of construction paper in half and staple through the papers on the fold. Create scenes from the book on the scrapbook pages.

Collage

Materials
- scissors
- old magazines
- glue
- construction paper

Cut out magazine pictures that represent different scenes from the story. Glue the pictures to a piece of construction paper. Write the title of the book at the top of your collage.

Riddles

Materials
- writing paper

Write five riddles about your book to share with the class.

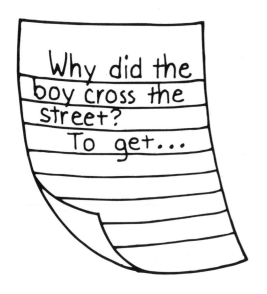

Storyteller

Materials
- none

Retell the story to the class or a group of students.

Literature Circles © 2001 Creative Teaching Press

Project Idea Cards

Diary

Materials
- writing paper
- stapler

Fold pieces of writing paper in half and staple through the papers on the fold. Choose a character from the book. Write numerous diary entries as if you were the character. Have the character comment on significant events in the story and thoughts about other characters.

Shadow Boxes

Materials
- scissors
- shoe box
- construction paper
- crayons or markers
- glue
- index card

Cut a quarter-sized hole in the side of a shoe box. Make three-dimensional figures out of construction paper and crayons or markers. Glue the figures to the inside bottom of the box. Replace the lid and look at the scene through the hole. Write a description of the scene on an index card. Glue the index card to the top of the box.

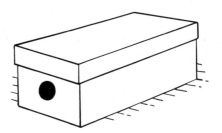

Bingo

Materials
- blank paper

Choose words that would describe events in the book. Create a Bingo game by drawing a game board and writing one word in each square. Write on a piece of paper a clue that describes each word.

Interview

Materials
- writing paper

Write questions for the author of your book. Have a member of your group pretend to be the author. Ask him or her to answer your interview questions. Write the answers on your paper.

Project Idea Cards

Picture Dictionary

Materials
- drawing paper
- stapler
- crayons or markers

Place several sheets of drawing paper together. Fold the paper in half and staple through the papers on the fold. Choose 20 interesting words from the book. Write each word at the top of a separate page. Draw a picture to represent the meaning of each word.

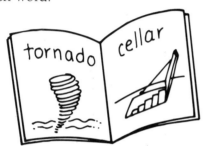

Poem

Materials
- paper

Write a haiku poem that describes the setting, a character, or the problem of the story. Structure your haiku to have three lines. Have five syllables on line one, seven syllables on line two, and five syllables on line three. Share your poem with the class.

> ### The Storm   Rob
>
> The trees were blowing.
> The big storm was on its way.
> The night air was crisp.

Song

Materials
- writing paper

Write a creative song about the characters in the story. Sing your song to the class.

Mobile

Materials
- scissors
- colored construction paper
- colored pencils, crayons, or markers
- tape
- string
- coat hanger

Cut assorted shapes from construction paper. Illustrate on a separate shape each of the following story elements in the book: the setting, the main characters, and the sequence of events. Write the title and author on a fourth shape. Tape each shape to a separate piece of string, and tape each string to a coat hanger to create a mobile.

Literature Circles © 2001 Creative Teaching Press

Literature Selections

Third Grade Literature

Key: = Advanced Reading   = Independent Reading   = Easy Reading

 Amber Brown Is Not a Crayon by Paula Danziger (Scholastic)

Amber Brown (whose name happens to be the color of a crayon) is a fourth grader who has a friend named Justin. The two friends have done everything together since preschool. Their friendship is challenged when Justin's dad gets a new job and his family has to move away. If that is not bad enough, Amber's parents are divorcing and her dad is taking a job in France. This story is about how Amber and Justin endure these changes and how friendship can survive. 80 pp. Realistic Fiction

 Be a Perfect Person in Just Three Days by Stephen Manes (Econo-Clad Books)

This is a very funny story about Milo Crinkley who longs to be perfect! While searching for a book in the library, he gets hit on the head by a book written by Dr. K. Pinkerton Silverfish called *Be A Perfect Person*. Milo spends the next three very difficult days following Dr. Silverfish's zany instructions and discovers being perfect is not all it is cut out to be. 76 pp. Fiction

 Bunnicula: A Rabbit Tale of Mystery by Deborah Howe (Simon & Schuster)

This is a hilarious story told from the perspective of a very literate dog, Harold, who lives with the Monroes and their also very literate cat, Chester. From the moment the Monroes find Bunnicula abandoned at a Dracula movie one rainy night and bring him home to keep, Chester is convinced Bunnicula is a vampire bunny and is determined to save the family from this harmless creature. Chester's wild imagination and misunderstood escapades hook the reader in until the very end. 98 pp. Fantasy

 Chocolate Fever by Robert Kimmel Smith (Econo-Clad Books)

Henry Green is a chocolate lover who can never get enough chocolate. One day, Henry discovers he is breaking out with brown spots and bumps—the first ever reported case of Chocolate Fever! Henry's love for chocolate results in him being placed in a hospital for examination, getting caught in a wild and silly chase, and encountering an unusual hijacking. 73 pp. Fiction

Chocolate Touch by Patrick Skene Catling (Econo-Clad Books)

John Midas finds a unique coin on the sidewalk and uses it to buy a box of chocolate. It's a chocolate lover's dream come true! As time passes, John discovers his life is getting more difficult. For example, when he kisses his mother she turns into chocolate. He soon realizes you should be careful what you wish for! 87 pp. Fiction

Class Clown by Johanna Hurwitz (Scholastic)

This story is about a hostile third-grade boy, Lucas Cott, who is always in trouble. He races his pencil, cracks jokes, and forgets to raise his hand in class. This story is full of humorous events that take place throughout the school year as Lucas tries to turn over a new leaf and become a model student. 98 pp. Realistic Fiction

The Courage of Sarah Noble by Alice Dalgliesh (Atheneum Books)

This story set in colonial America demonstrates the courage and bravery needed to survive in 1701. Sarah Noble and her father journey through the wilderness to build a new home for their family. When her father leaves her alone in the wilderness while he returns for the rest of the family, Sarah must learn not to be afraid as she befriends her Indian neighbors. She learns that bravery is the greatest courage of all. 54 pp. Historical Fiction

Dear Mr. Henshaw by Beverly Cleary (William Morrow & Company)

In this story, a young boy, Leigh Botts, begins writing to his favorite author, Mr. Henshaw, during a very difficult time in his life. His parents are divorced, he lives in a very small house, and his dad, a truck driver, has taken his dog with him. Through his correspondence with Mr. Henshaw, Leigh deals with his feelings and learns to accept himself. 134 pp. Realistic Fiction

Freckle Juice by Judy Blume (Econo-Clad Books)

In this humorous story, Andrew wants to have freckles in the worst way. He thinks that if he has freckles, his mom would not be able to tell if his neck is dirty. Sharon, one of his classmates, knows of his wish and offers him her secret recipe for Freckle Juice. When this recipe makes Andrew sick, he takes matters into his own hands and puts magic marker freckles on his face. 47 pp. Realistic Fiction

How to Eat Fried Worms by Thomas Rockwell (Yearling Books)

Ten-year-old Billy would like to buy the mini-bike of his dreams and finds himself in the predicament of eating 15 worms in 15 days! Billy's friends create a variety of appetizing ways to serve these creatures so he can earn the prize of $50.00 and a brand-new mini-bike. This irresistible story is filled with twists and turns. 116 pp. Fiction

Howliday Inn by James Howe (Atheneum Books)

This hilarious story of a dog and cat duo from the Bunnicula series takes place when the Monroe family goes on vacation and leaves Harold and Chester at the Chateau Bow Wow. While there, the two find themselves in the middle of a mystery—the disappearance of Louise, a French poodle. Chester believes any one of the six other guests is capable of this crime, and the two set out to discover who did it! 195 pp. Fantasy

The Kid Who Only Hit Homers by Matt Christopher (Little, Brown and Company)

This baseball story is about a boy named Sylvester. Sylvester goes from being a poor hitter to a boy who hits only homers after he meets a mysterious character, George Baruth. Sylvester now has to deal with all the troubling questions about his new-found talent and learn to deal with his sudden fame. 127 pp. Fiction

Marvin Redpost: Kidnapped at Birth? by Louis Sachar (Econo-Clad Books)

This is a funny story about a third-grade boy, Marvin, who writes a current event on the King of Shampoon who is looking for his son. Marvin is convinced that the reason he does not look like anyone in his family is because he was kidnapped at birth. He believes he is Robert, the lost prince of Shampoon! 80 pp. Realistic Fiction

The Minpins by Roald Dahl (Viking)

In this picture book, little Billy disobeys his mother and wanders into the "Forest of Sin." Billy discovers the magical world of miniature people called Minpins who own the forest, live in tree cities (hollow trees filled with rooms and staircases), and fly on the backs of birds to get where they want to go. When Billy learns that the red-hot smoke-belching Gruncher is terrorizing them, he forms a plan to lure the monster away and becomes their hero! 47 pp. Fantasy

Miss Rumphius by Barbara Cooney (Econo-Clad Books)

As a small child, Alice Rumphius told her grandfather that when she grew up she would go to faraway places and live beside the sea. Her grandfather tells her that there is a third thing she must do as well. She must make the world a beautiful place. In this story, readers find out if a grown-up Miss Rumphius accomplished these three things. 32 pp. Fiction

Molly's Pilgrim by Barbara Cohen (Lothrop Lee & Shepard)

A young Jewish Russian immigrant, Molly, is struggling to adjust to school in America. When Molly learns about the first American Thanksgiving from her teacher, she in turn teaches her classmates a very poignant lesson on pilgrims. 32 pp. Historical Fiction

(A) *The Mouse and the Motorcycle* by Beverly Cleary (William Morrow & Company)

Ralph, a mouse, lives in a knothole in a hotel room of the Mountain View Inn. When a family checks into the hotel, Ralph gets his chance to ride his very own toy motorcycle. Ralph's adventures lead to trouble, but in the end he goes on a life-saving adventure. 172 pp. Fantasy

(E) *The One in the Middle Is the Green Kangaroo* by Judy Blume (Atheneum Books)

This is a story about a boy named Freddy Dissel who always feels left out and dislikes being the middle child in his family. Freddy's feelings change when he gets to play the part of a green kangaroo in a school play and he shows people just how special he really is. 39 pp. Realistic Fiction

(I) *Ramona the Brave* by Beverly Cleary (William Morrow & Company)

Six-year-old Ramona Quimby is determined to be as brave as possible as she deals with all the changes in her life. As Ramona enters first grade, she must deal with her mom's return to work, sleeping alone in her new bedroom, a copycat in her class, and a fierce dog on the sidewalk. Spunky little Ramona deals with all of these adventures in her own humorous way! 190 pp. Realistic Fiction

(A) *Sarah, Plain and Tall* by Patricia MacLachlan (HarperCollins)

In this story, a widowed Midwestern farmer named Jacob Witting and his two children, Anna and Caleb, put an ad in the paper asking for a wife and mother. When Sarah Elizabeth Wheaton arrives from Maine for a month and gets to know the family, she changes their lives forever. 58 pp. Historical Fiction

(A) *Shiloh* by Phyllis Reynolds Naylor (Aladdin)

Eleven-year-old Marty Preston finds a young beagle (Shiloh) while out walking in the hills of Friendly, West Virginia. Marty suspects the pup is mistreated and hides Shiloh from his parents and his owner. It doesn't take long for Marty to fall in love with Shiloh and do whatever it takes to keep the pup as his own despite the difficulties he has with the dog's owner. 226 pp. Realistic Fiction

(I) *The Spy on Third Base* by Matt Christopher (Little, Brown and Company)

In this story, third baseman T. V. Adams has the ability to know exactly where the batters will hit the ball. T. V. must decide whether or not he should use his talent to help his team. 62 pp. Fiction

(E) ***Sweet Clara and the Freedom Quilt*** by Deborah Hopkinson (Knopf)

Eleven-year-old Clara is a slave on the Home Plantation. While working in the Big House, she saves scraps of colorful cloth for a quilt that becomes a map depicting the route of the Underground Railroad and a way north to freedom. When Clara finally escapes, she leaves the quilt behind for others to use. 32 pp. Historical Fiction

(E) ***Through Grandpa's Eyes*** by Patricia MacLachlan (HarperCollins)

In this story, Grandpa shares his enjoyment of life with his grandson, John. When John does not understand how Grandpa sees and moves about in the world, Grandpa shares his secrets with John. 40 pp. Fiction

(I) ***The Velveteen Rabbit*** by Margery Williams Bianco (Doubleday Books)

A young boy receives a stuffed rabbit for Christmas. Since the day the Skin Horse in the nursery tells the rabbit about being real, the velveteen rabbit dreams of the day when he will become real. 32 pp. Fantasy

Fourth Grade Literature

Key: **(A)** = Advanced Reading   **(I)** = Independent Reading   **(E)** = Easy Reading

(A) *Babe—The Gallant Pig* by Dick King-Smith (Crown Books)

This book is about a pig named Babe who "becomes" a sheepdog, following in the footsteps of his foster mother, Fly, a sheepdog for Farmer Hogget. Babe learns to treat the "stupid" animals with manners and respect. 128 pp. Fantasy

(A) *The Best School Year Ever* by Barbara Robinson (HarperCollins)

This book tells the story of the Herdmans, the worst kids in the entire town, who always manage to escape being caught. A school assignment teaches everyone that there is some good in everybody. 117 pp. Realistic Fiction

(I) *Charlie and the Chocolate Factory* by Roald Dahl (Knopf)

When five children win a tour through Willy Wonka's mysterious chocolate factory, greed stands in the way for all but one child, Charlie. 155 pp. Fantasy

(A) *Charlotte's Web* by E. B. White (HarperCollins)

This story is about a special friendship between a pig named Wilbur and a spider named Charlotte. Charlotte saves Wilbur from certain slaughter by spinning a web that reads "Some Pig," causing the humans to believe Wilbur is special. 184 pp. Fantasy

(A) *The Cricket in Times Square* by George Seldon (Farrar, Straus & Giroux)

The adventures begin when a very talented musical cricket finds himself in a Times Square subway station. The cricket learns the lessons of friendship, sacrifice, and the price of fame. 160 pp. Fantasy

(E) *Fantastic Mr. Fox* by Roald Dahl (Econo-Clad Books)

In this story, three horrible farmers have one objective: to get rid of the fantastic Mr. Fox. Mr. Fox not only saves himself but saves all the animals in his community. 81 pp. Fantasy

(A) *Homer Price* by Robert McCloskey (Viking)

This book about the life of Homer Price, his small town neighbors, friends, and family is a refreshing look at America. It is divided into six exciting episodes. One episode is about the capture of four bandits. 149 pp. Realistic Fiction

(E) *The Hundred Penny Box* by Sharon Bell Mathis (Viking)

This is the story of a hundred-year-old woman and her box of 100 pennies, one for each year of her life. Each penny holds the memory of the year it represented. The one person who understands the woman and her pennies, her great-great-nephew, creates a special bond between old and young. 48 pp. Realistic Fiction

(A) *The Indian in the Cupboard* by Lynne Reid Banks (Doubleday Books)

A small cabinet and an old key combine to magically bring plastic toys to life. Omri, a young child, watches the adventure of a lifetime as he witnesses not mere toys but actual people. 184 pp. Fantasy

(I) *Island of the Blue Dolphins* by Scott O'Dell (Houghton Mifflin)

This is a story of survival and self-preservation as a young girl remains stranded alone on an island for 18 years. 192 pp. Historical Fiction

(A) *James and the Giant Peach* by Roald Dahl (Knopf)

James, a young boy, becomes an orphan when his parents are killed in an accident and he must live with two wicked old aunts. Some magic crystals cause a giant peach to grow, which eventually carries James away on some wild adventures. 126 pp. Fantasy

(I) *Little House on the Prairie* by Laura Ingalls Wilder (HarperCollins)

This book is about a little girl named Laura and her family. Together they travel west in a covered wagon, looking for a new place to settle. An unfortunate circumstance causes them to have to move again once settled. This book is filled with historical details, such as the building of a log cabin and the pioneer way of celebrating Christmas. 335 pp. Nonfiction

(I) *Mr. Popper's Penguins* by Richard Atwater (Little, Brown and Company)

This book tells the tale of a poor housepainter, Mr. Popper, who receives a penguin as a gift from a polar explorer to whom he wrote a fan letter. One penguin soon becomes twelve and Mr. Popper needs to raise money to support his brood. 139 pp. Fiction

(I) *Night of the Twisters* by Ivy Ruckman (HarperCollins)

Dan Hatch, a twelve-year-old boy, his best friend, and Dan's baby brother are alone in the house when a tornado hits Grand Island. Read about the boys' bravery and their quick thinking, which helps them survive their ordeal. 153 pp. Fiction

(I) *Pigs Might Fly* by Dick King-Smith (Puffin)

The runt of the litter, "Daggie Dogfoot," was born on a pig farm in England. Daggie overhears that "pigs might fly" and sets out to learn to fly. Learning to fly leads Daggie to learn to swim. This becomes useful when a fierce rainstorm bursts the dam, causing most of the farm to flood. Daggie comes to the rescue by swimming for help. 158 pp. Fiction

(A) *The Sign of the Beaver* by Elizabeth George Speare (Houghton Mifflin)

This book is about the friendship and respect that develop between Matt, a young white boy, and Attean, a young Indian boy. Both boys learn to value and respect the differences in each other's cultures. 144 pp. Historical Fiction

(A) *Skinnybones* by Barbara Park (Econo-Clad Books)

Wisecracking Alex "Skinnybones" Frankovich gets more than he bargains for when he takes on the baseball team's star pitcher. 131 pp. Fiction

(I) *Stone Fox* by John Reynolds Gardiner (HarperCollins)

This is a story about ten-year-old Willy. He enters a dogsled race to try and win money to pay the taxes on his family's farm. His major competition, Stone Fox and his team of dogs, have never lost a race before. 96 pp. Realistic Fiction

(A) *Stuart Little* by E. B. White (HarperTrophy)

This book tells the story of Stuart Little, a mouse born into a human family in New York City, much to the dismay of the mean family cat. 131 pp. Fantasy

(E) *A Taste of Blackberries* by Doris Buchanan Smith (HarperCollins)

Jamie and his best friend are young boys living in a small town. One day, tragedy strikes, leaving Jamie's best friend to cope with the tragedy. At the same time, he is left trying to understand how life can go on without Jamie. 64 pp. Fiction

(I) *There's a Boy in the Girls' Bathroom* by Louis Sachar (Random House)

Bradley Chalkers, a fifth grader with poor social skills, considers himself an outcast. He eventually learns to trust others when he makes a new friend and works with the school counselor who helps him find the good inside himself. 195 pp. Realistic Fiction

(A) *War Comes to Willy Freeman* by James Lincoln Collier and Christopher Collier (Yearling Books)

Willy is a thirteen-year-old free black girl who watches the redcoats kill her father in Revolutionary War Connecticut. She sets out, disguised as a boy, to find her mother. 192 pp. Historical Fiction

The War with Grandpa by Robert Kimmel Smith (Yearling Books)

Peter is excited when Grandpa comes to live with his family until he finds out that Grandpa is taking his room. Peter is forced to move upstairs and a war with his grandpa begins that includes playing many funny tricks on each other. 160 pp. Realistic Fiction

 The Whipping Boy by Sid Fleischman (William Morrow & Company)

In this book, the orphaned Jemmy is taken to the palace to receive the whippings for "Prince Brat," a spoiled rotten heir to the throne. Both boys run away and end up together. 90 pp. Historical Fiction

The Witches by Roald Dahl (Farrar, Straus & Giroux)

An orphaned boy goes to live with his grandmother and learns about real witches, the kind that look like ordinary women but hate children. A special bond is created between the boy and his grandmother. 208 pp. Fantasy

A Wrinkle in Time by Madeline L'Engle (Farrar, Straus & Giroux)

Meg finds out her father, a gifted scientist, is a prisoner on another planet. She, along with her brilliant younger brother, travel through a tesseract, a wrinkle in time and space, to rescue their father. 211 pp. Science Fiction

Fifth Grade Literature

Key: (A) = Advanced Reading   (I) = Independent Reading   (E) = Easy Reading

(I) ***The Best Christmas Pageant Ever*** by Barbara Robinson (HarperCollins)

In this book, the Herdman children, generally regarded as the worst kids in town, take over the community Christmas pageant. What happens next is both unexpected and humorous. 80 pp. Fiction

(E) ***The Big Wave*** by Pearl S. Buck (HarperCollins)

This story is about a young Japanese boy who loses his family to a tidal wave. After the disaster, Jiya must learn to go on with his life. 57 pp. Fiction

(I) ***Bridge to Terabithia*** by Katherine Paterson (HarperCollins)

This book is about a boy and a girl who become best friends after a fifth-grade race. Jess and Leslie create a special sanctuary in the woods called Terabithia. Here the two friends grow closer until Leslie's death. 144 pp. Fiction

(I) ***Call It Courage*** by Armstrong Sperry (Simon & Schuster)

Mafatu is the son of the great chief of the people of his island. All his life he has been afraid of the sea, but he decides to face his fears and sets out on his own to find the courage within himself. 95 pp. Fiction

(E) ***The Cybil War*** by Betsy Byars (Viking)

Simon and Tony are best friends until Cybil comes into the picture. Simon realizes that fifth grade becomes much more complicated when love is a part of it. 112 pp. Fiction

(A) ***The Devil's Arithmetic*** by Jane Yolen (Econo-Clad Books)

Hannah Stern is a twelve-year-old girl who is transported back in time to the 1940s in Poland. She experiences firsthand how it felt to be in a concentration camp during the Holocaust. 170 pp. Historical Fiction

(I) ***The Dollhouse Murders*** by Betty Ren Wright (Scholastic)

Twelve-year-old Amy discovers an old-fashioned dollhouse in her aunt's attic. She soon learns that the dolls in the dollhouse are giving her clues to a 30-year-old double murder mystery. 160 pp. Mystery

The Enormous Egg by Oliver Butterworth (Econo-Clad Books)

In this book, twelve-year-old Nate finds an enormous egg in his family's henhouse. He is determined to see it hatch, but he never expects the egg to contain a triceratops. 188 pp. Fiction

Hatchet by Gary Paulsen (Econo-Clad Books)

Thirteen-year-old Brian is the sole survivor of a single engine plane crash in the Canadian wilderness. He learns to keep himself alive with the use of his hatchet and his own knowledge and resourcefulness. 195 pp. Adventure

The Lion, the Witch, and the Wardrobe by C. S. Lewis (Econo-Clad Books)

Four English children discover an enchanted world called Narnia when they step through a wardrobe. They attempt to return in the spring to Narnia and break the spell on the white witch. 206 pp. Fantasy

The Midnight Fox by Betsy Byars (Econo-Clad Books)

Tom, an angry ten-year-old boy, is spending the summer on his aunt's farm while his parents travel to Europe. Tom's anger disappears when he discovers a black fox and begins to follow the fox's life. 134 pp. Fiction

Number the Stars by Lois Lowry (Houghton Mifflin)

This story takes place in Denmark in 1943. Annemarie and Ellen are both ten-year-old girls. Annemarie's family harbors Ellen to protect her from the Nazi soldiers. Annemarie must be courageous to help smuggle Ellen and her parents out of the country. 137 pp. Historical Fiction

Old Yeller by Fred Gipson (HarperCollins)

Fourteen-year-old Travis learns to love an ugly, yellow dog. The two of them protect the family and have many adventures together in the Texas wilderness. Travis must kill his beloved dog after Old Yeller is bitten by a rabid wolf. 192 pp. Fiction

The Phantom Tollbooth by Norton Juster (Random House)

Milo is a bored ten-year-old who embarks upon a fantastic journey towards Dictionopolis. He is accompanied by a watchdog named Tock. Together they set off to rescue the twin princesses, Rhyme and Reason. 255 pp. Fantasy

The Pushcart War by Jean Merrill (Econo-Clad Books)

The pushcart peddlers and the truck drivers of New York City declare a war between themselves in 1976. Both groups are determined to rid the crowded streets of the other group. The pushcart peddlers begin to employ peashooters to help them in this battle. 224 pp. Fiction

(I) *The Riddle of Penncroft Farm* by Dorothea Jensen (Harcourt)

In this story, Lars moves from Minnesota to his great-aunt's farm, which happens to be near Valley Forge in Pennsylvania. He becomes friends with the ghost of an eighteenth-century ancestor who shares his stories from the time of the Revolutionary War. 192 pp. Historical Fiction

(E) *Sadako and the Thousand Paper Cranes* by Eleanor Coerr (Puffin)

Ten-year-old Sadako was two years old when the atomic bomb was dropped on Hiroshima, Japan. She develops the "atom bomb disease," leukemia, and turns to folding a thousand paper cranes with the wish to be well again. 80 pp. Nonfiction

(A) *The Secret Garden* by Frances Hodgson Burnett (HarperCollins)

Orphaned Mary Lennox comes to England to live with her uncle and sickly cousin, Colin. Mary, Colin, and a friend named Dickon discover a locked garden. The children learn to care for the garden and for each other. 85 pp. Fiction

(A) *Summer of the Swans* by Betsy Byars (Econo-Clad Books)

This book is about a girl named Sara who has a mentally retarded brother, Charlie. Charlie wanders towards the lake when he hears some swans and becomes lost. Sara's search for Charlie causes her to search within herself and her feelings. 144 pp. Fiction

(A) *Traitor: The Case of Benedict Arnold* by Jean Fritz (Econo-Clad Books)

This book studies the life and character of Benedict Arnold, a brilliant Revolutionary War general. It focuses on his betrayal and the aftermath of his treason. 192 pp. Nonfiction

(A) *Wait Till Helen Comes: A Ghost Story* by Mary Downing Hahn (Avon Books)

Molly, a twelve-year-old, dislikes her stepsister Heather but realizes she must protect her when a ghost named Helen tries to take the two girls into her world. 184 pp. Fiction

(A) *The Westing Game* by Ellen Raskin (Dutton)

This story is a mystery about Sam Westing's murder. Sam gives out clues in his will to help his heirs try to identify the murderer. His heirs must solve the mystery before they can claim their inheritance. 216 pp. Mystery

(I) *The Witch of Blackbird Pond* by Elizabeth George Speare (Houghton Mifflin)

The year is 1687 and Kit is a Puritan orphan who comes to stay with her aunt and uncle in Connecticut. Kit has trouble fitting in as she rebels against the narrow-mindedness of her community. Kit befriends an old woman who is later accused of being a witch. 249 pp. Historical Fiction

Sixth Grade Literature

Key: = Advanced Reading   = Independent Reading   (E) = Easy Reading

(I)   ***Black Star, Bright Dawn*** by Scott O'Dell (Houghton Mifflin)

When her father is injured while training for the Iditarod (the famous 1,200 mile dogsled race between Anchorage and Nome), 18-year-old Bright Dawn must take over his position as the village's dog racer. She is befriended by an older Eskimo who gives her advice and reminds her of the wisdom of her people. 103 pp. Realistic Fiction

(A)   ***The Cay*** by Theodore Taylor (Random House)

During World War II, a young white boy and an old black man are stranded on a small Caribbean island when the freighter they are traveling on is torpedoed by a German submarine. The boy, Phillip, is blinded by a blow to the head but discovers that although he has no vision, he can now truly "see" his own stereotypes and prejudices. Timothy, his old companion, teaches him many things, from survival skills to acceptance of people who are different. 144 pp. Historical Fiction

(I)   ***Death on the Nile*** by Agatha Christie (HarperCollins)

A young and beautiful woman named Linnet Doyle takes a cruise on the Nile with her husband and finds herself caught in a baffling mystery. Hercule Poirot, a private detective, investigates the murder on the cruise ship. 320 pp. Mystery

(I)   ***The Egypt Game*** by Zilpha Keatley Snyder (Atheneum)

A group of children turn a deserted lot into an imaginary Egypt where they play their own Egypt game. They enact rituals, consult oracles, become involved in a murder, and befriend a professor. Their fantasy game leads to strange, inexplicable happenings and their game almost comes to a disastrous end. 240 pp. Fantasy/Mystery

(E)   ***Everyone Else's Parents Said Yes*** by Paula Danziger (Econo-Clad Books)

Matthew Martin is an annoying soon-to-be eleven-year-old boy. He regularly insults his sister and plays embarrassing jokes on his classmates. Meanwhile, he is eagerly anticipating his birthday party—a sleep-over with tons of junk food. He finds that he must face the consequences for his behavior when the sixth-grade girls declare war on him and it coincides with his party. 126 pp. Realistic Fiction

(E)   ***The Fledgling*** by Jane Langton (HarperTrophy)

Georgie Hall wants nothing more than to be able to fly and a Canadian goose helps her to realize her dreams. 182 pp. Fantasy

(E) *Gentle Ben* by Walt Morey (Puffin)

Set in the rugged Alaskan territory, this is the story of a boy named Mark and a bear named Ben who become friends. When Mark's older brother dies, he finds himself drawn to the huge bear, which is chained up by its owner. Mark and Ben form a unique bond, and the boy is able to save the bear from an untimely demise. 192 pp. Realistic Fiction

(A) *The Golden Goblet* by Eloise Jarvis McGraw (Econo-Clad Books)

Ranofer, a young Egyptian boy, is orphaned and taken in by his malicious and thieving older half-brother. Ranofer's life ambition is to be a master goldsmith, but his brother beats him and forces him to be an apprentice in his stonecutting shop. Ranofer struggles to reveal his brother's true nature and reshape his own future. 248 pp. Historical Fiction

(I) *The Great Gilly Hopkins* by Katherine Paterson (HarperTrophy)

An eleven-year-old girl in foster care struggles to belong. Whenever people try to reach out to her, she schemes against them. Just when her social worker is about to give up, Gilly is placed with a new foster family. Gilly tries to cope with her unhappiness throughout the story. 148 pp. Realistic Fiction

(I) *The Incredible Journey* by Sheila Burnford (Laurel-Leaf Books)

Separated from their owners, a Siamese cat, an old bull terrier, and a young Labrador retriever travel 250 miles through the Canadian wilderness in order to return to their home. Instinct guides them through dangerous wilderness and they must rely on each other in order to survive many challenges. 145 pp. Fiction

(I) *Maniac Magee* by Jerry Spinelli (Little, Brown and Company)

This tall tale is a story about race relations. Jeffrey "Maniac" Magee is a white boy who has lost his parents in a tragic accident. He runs away to Two Mills, a town sharply divided by the white West End and the black East End. It is here that he becomes a legend, helps bridge the gap between the two sides of the town, and finds a place to call home. 192 pp. Legend/Fiction

(I) *Mara—Daughter of the Nile* by Eloise Jarvis McGraw (Econo-Clad Books)

Set in ancient Egypt during the days when Queen Hatshepsut ruled, this story is about a young Egyptian slave girl who spies in the royal palace of Thebes. She is a double spy for two archenemies and when this is discovered, her life is at stake. 279 pp. Historical Fiction